I0813133

BIG CATS

COUGARS

by Elizabeth Andrews

Cody Koala
An Imprint of Pop!
popbooksonline.com

Hello! My name is Cody Koala

This book is filled with videos, puzzles, games, and more! Scan the QR codes* while you read, or visit the website below to make this book pop.

popbooksonline.com/cougar

*Scanning QR codes requires a web-enabled smart device with a QR code reader app and a camera.

abdobooks.com
Published by Pop!, a division of ABDO, PO Box 398166, Minneapolis, Minnesota 55439.

Printed in the United States of America, North Mankato, Minnesota.
102024
012025

Cover Photo: Shutterstock Images
Interior Photos: Getty Images, Shutterstock Images
Editor: Grace Hansen
Series Designer: Neil Klinepier, Candice Keimig

Library of Congress Control Number: 2024938594

Publisher's Cataloging-in-Publication Data
Names: Andrews, Elizabeth, author.
Title: Cougars / by Elizabeth Andrews
Description: Minneapolis, Minnesota : Pop!, 2025 | Series: Big cats | Includes online resources and index
Identifiers: ISBN 9781098246891 (lib. bdg.) | ISBN 9781098247454 (ebook)
Subjects: LCSH: Big cats--Juvenile literature. | Wildcat--Juvenile literature. | Puma--Juvenile literature. | Cougar--Juvenile literature. | Puma--Behavior--Juvenile literature.
Classification: DDC 599.755--dc23

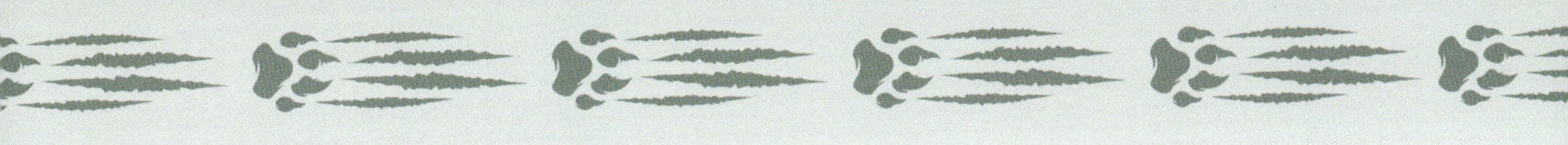

Table of Contents

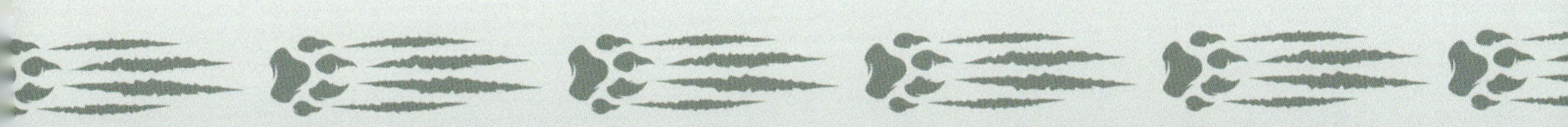

Chapter 1

What Is a Cougar?

A cougar is a large cat. Cougars are also called pumas and mountain lions. Their size depends on where they live. Cougars are smaller in warmer **habitats**. They are larger in colder habitats.

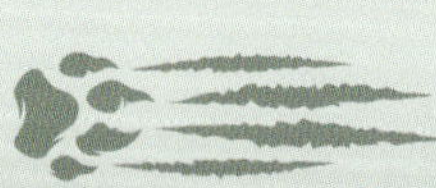

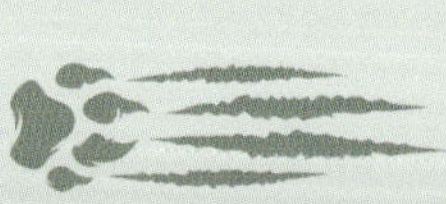

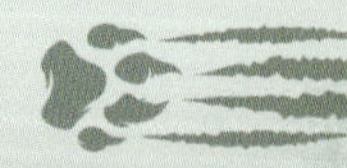

Cougars can swim, but they don't like being wet!

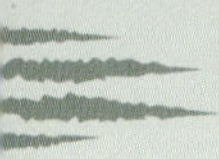

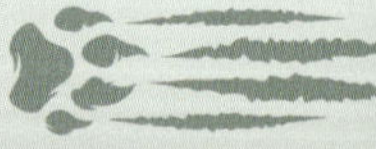

Cougars have thick fur. Depending on the season, the fur can be reddish, grayish, or brownish in color. Cougars don't have any special markings. They have large eyes and good eyesight.

Cougars are sturdy animals. They have large paws and strong legs.

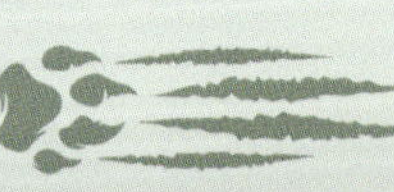
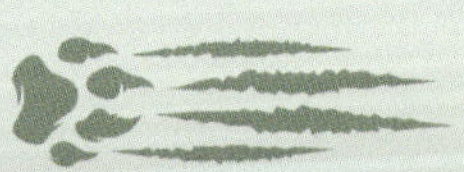

Their back legs are longer than their front legs. They can jump 20 feet (6.1m)!

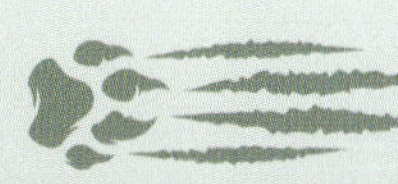
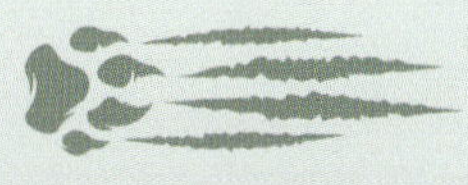
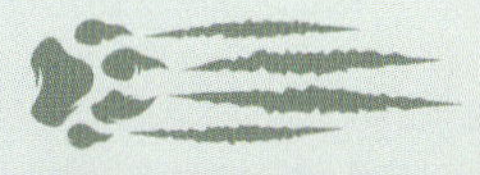

Chapter 2

Where Do Cougars Live?

Cougars can be found as far north as Alaska all the way down to Chile and Argentina. Cougars live in many different **habitats**. They live in wetlands, forests, deserts, and mountains.

Where Cougars Live

North America
Europe
Atlantic Ocean
Africa
South America
Pacific Ocean
N W E S
Cougar Range

Learn more here!

 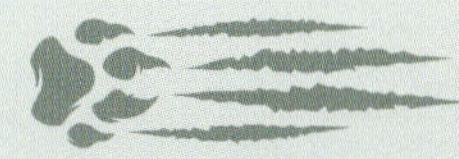 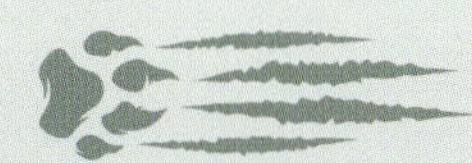  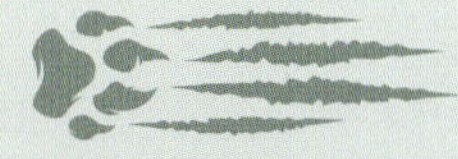

Chapter 3

Cougar Habits

Cougars cannot roar like other big cats. They hiss, growl, purr, and whistle to communicate. Cougars rest in thick brush, rocky **crevices**, and caves during the day. They hunt at night.

Explore links here!

Cougars hide their kill and feed on it for a few days.

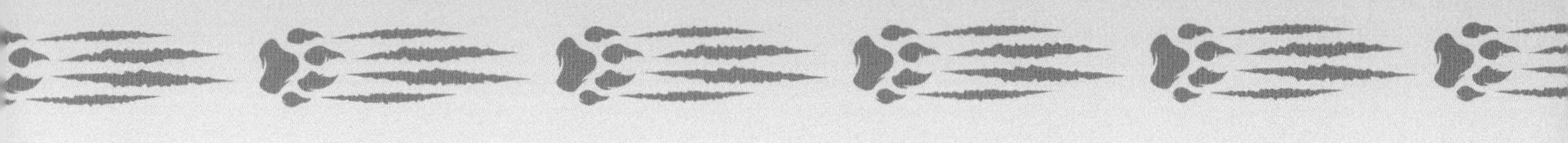

Cougars are **carnivores**. Their large eyes help them hunt at night. Cougars sneak up to and pounce on their **prey**. They mostly eat small mammals such as raccoons and armadillos. They sometimes eat larger animals such as elk.

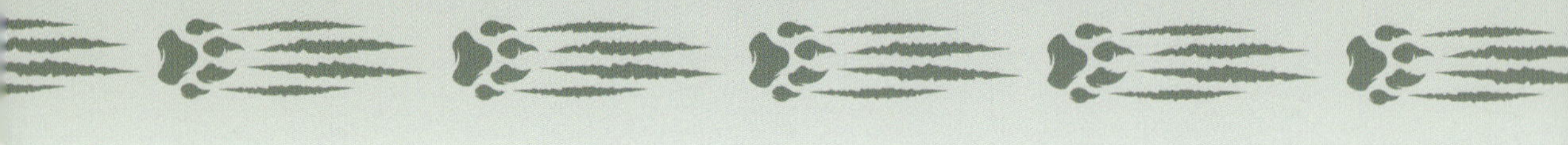

Cougars are **solitary** animals. Each adult cougar has a **territory** that it lives and hunts in. The territories of female cougars sometimes overlap. Males do not share territory with other males.

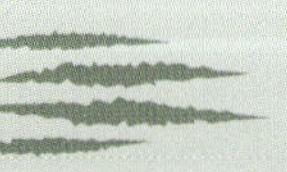
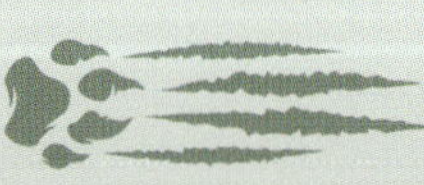
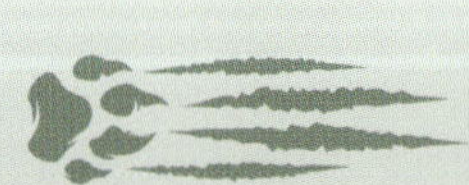

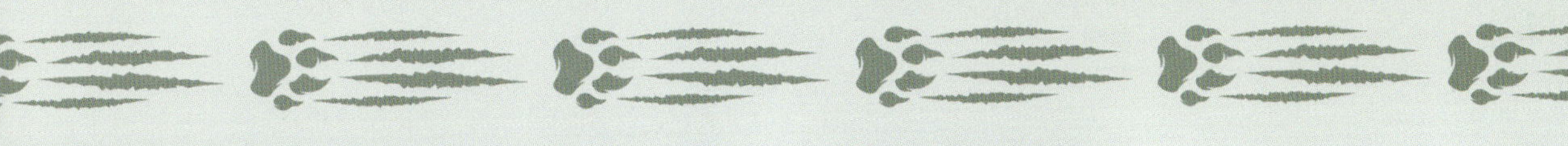

Chapter 4

Cougar Cubs

Female cougars have one to six cubs at a time. Cubs are born with spots. The spots help them blend into the forest floor when their mother leaves them to hunt.

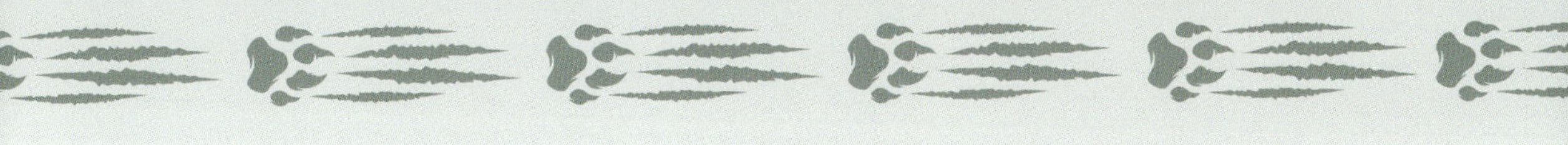

Complete an activity here!

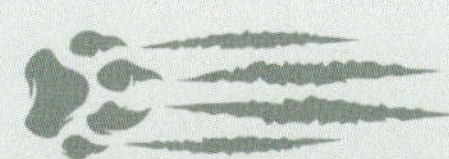

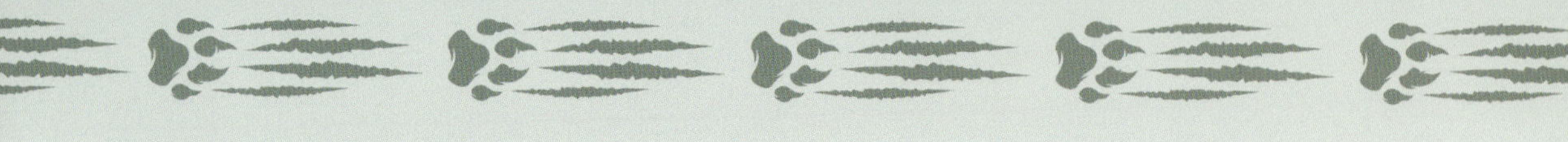

Cougars sometimes travel six miles (9.6km) at night to find food.

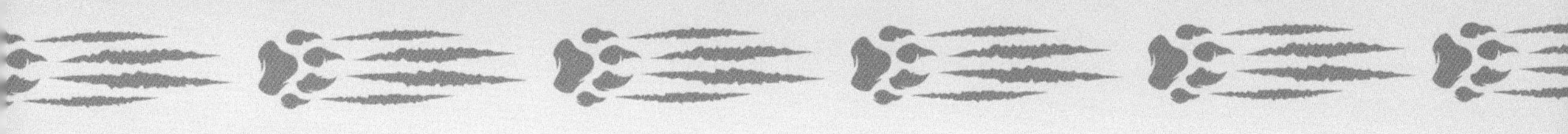

Cubs stay with their mother for two years. They start eating meat at six weeks old. Their mother teaches them how to hunt. Male cougars usually live to be 13 years old. Female cougars usually live to be 16.

Making Connections

Text-to-Self

What big cat are you most interested in? Please explain your answer.

Text-to-Text

Have you read about any other kinds of big cats? If so, how were those big cats similar to or different from cougars?

Text-to-World

Cougar cubs have markings to help them hide. Can you think of any other cubs or baby animals that have markings that help them hide?

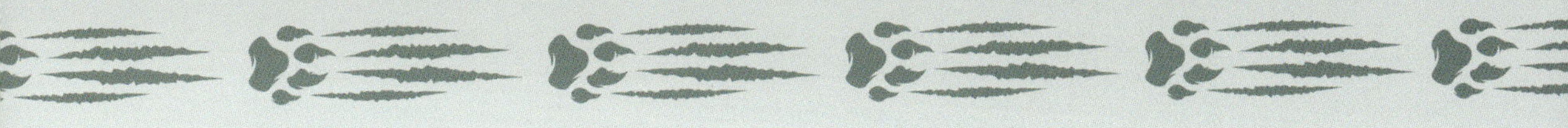

Glossary

carnivore – an animal that feeds on other animals.

crevice – a narrow opening usually formed by a split or crack.

habitat – the home of an animal.

prey – an animal that is hunted by other animals for food.

solitary – living alone.

territory – a particular area of land that belongs to an animal.

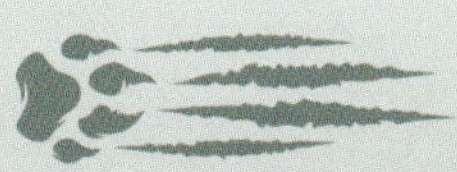
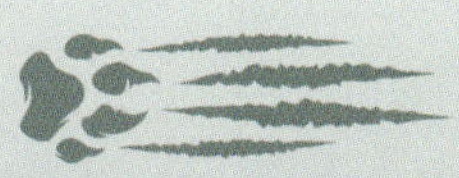
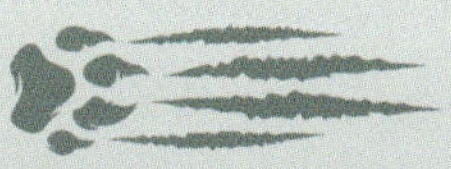

Index

Online Resources

popbooksonline.com

Thanks for reading this Cody Koala book!

This book is filled with videos, puzzles, games, and more! Scan the QR codes* while you read, or visit the website below to make this book pop.

popbooksonline.com/cougar

*Scanning QR codes requires a web-enabled smart device with a QR code reader app and a camera.